VOLUME V
The Altar Collective

Volume V:
an anthology of short stories

The Altar Collective was created in 2013
by Katherine Hogan

www.thealtarcollective.com

Cover and interior art by Amy Goh
(http://kuroneko.yolasite.com/)
Logo art by Anthony Lopez

Special thanks to Sean Moor, Gatsby Books

CONTENTS

Destroy Yourself

1.

She is looking at me. The most beautiful woman of antiquity is looking at me. It almost hurts, her gaze, so David's marble-carved scrutiny will too be made sharp when the vines begin to tear at his unblemished complexion. Yet, it is not direct. I am moved. I stagger away from the canvas with trembling steps and indeed she does not face me, though there is something of a mirror that facilitates all reciprocity. Nevertheless it is not her gaze, no, not the invisible impress that moves me. Her face is turned and even the mirror cannot justly recreate her divine countenance as if even Velázquez, displaying a grimace of dread and wonder, could not bear her sight. Perhaps similarly I would be smote upon seeing that dreadful and profound goddess, as well kept of a secret as de León's lucidity. The only palpable element that is available to me is the linear fluidity that shapes her back of white canvas, the curve Matisse etched with a single stroke. Alas, the mirror invites me into dialogue, but cannot re-create the scene, but beauty as the first cause, the creator, COMPULSIVE, beauty that moves me, resolves my blood to molten gold, the pure potentiality of beauty gilds me into the portrait, brush in one hand, knife in the other.

An alternative: although you can never truly comprehend the other, substantiate your existence by laying her gaze upon you.

She has seen so much and been seen – however false – by so many and now her gaze has fallen upon me. Velázquez she saw as he introduced the goddess to her final inhabitancy of the sublunary realm – his inquisitive grasp of the caked palette, his frailty. She saw, too, the basement inventory of Spain's already setting Golden Age – though never the sun. As revolt, bankruptcy, and plague ravaged the Hapsburgs, she saw only the inquisitor curate, selecting those canvases to be hung on the court's walls and those to be hanged in the court's fires, the pigment sparking colored flames of hues known only to those primal alchemists who, in a flash of smoke, discovered and destroyed their secrets. Was the same demeanor – languid, demure – then reflected upon faithful Cupid's whetted mirror? Did a single gasp perhaps escape unseen from between her pouted lips when Mrs. Mary Suffragette slashed at her virgin skin? Does she blush even now when insufferable men like me molest her the same with hazy eyes and mouths agape? After everything we have all shared the same line of sight.

It was the work of a master who could make solid the invisible. It is the work of a terrorist or god to stand inert beneath the tortuous veil of beauty. The latter will no longer be sufficient to complete the first. I will achieve what Paris himself was unable even to desire; I will seize the god. The offerings of the triumvirate are without worth measured by the wisdom of necessity, which is only available in reflection, and our own fate seems to be realized the moment we believe it to be true. Suggesting to make us whole like they are in a game of vanity and mockery – complete with a coy twist of the lip –, the gods gave us the deceptive ability to possess beauty, a gift that has plagued us ever since. To hell with our god-given inalienable blindness: our endeavors to understand the mechanics of the great tapestry that circumscribes the universe in a single act of creation are only in vain if the fabric is unwoven before our pathetic little kneeling selves. If it is not, our procreation becomes the machine by which Borges is empowered to kill the gods who are not so terrible as to exist.

The foam of the Lady Cyprus' birth is frothing at my mouth. No, this is not the lunatic's castration – the orchid that Linnaeus doubtless plucked grows ever at my feet entwining this horrid stance and obscuring my gaze. Love moves me now to my knees – yes, I can call it love, for that great impulse is always a paltry reaction. I pray as a suppliant to the rosy-fingered goddess that she might look away from my depraved corpse, I who gave her life, as I cannot bear to shred this ethereal bond. I am unable to initiate any possibility that will

9

threaten my humble temple lest it fail to contain the gears that turn yet the heavenly spheres. Perhaps I am unable. The very act of knowing is perpetually false. For Socrates, beauty exists only in his false denouncement of life that implies a better form. My dull imaginings cannot even suggest beauty. Being in life cannot know death; being in time cannot fathom the future or past or all other infinities. I thought I could create it in velleity. We are only half-beings that I will make whole in action by destroying what tortures me. *Mirrors: which scoop up the beauty that has streamed from their face and gathers it back, into themselves, entire* – no longer.

How terrible a notion that I who never wanted a mask will sit inert beneath the ornate ringlets of gold that flourish this frame and not one oblivious voyeur will see a man consumed by the vines of dust and snakes that silently gather unnoticed in the corner. Is that a crime? Undoubtedly most stiff-collared visitors smile at lovely Aphrodite's disproportioned reflection and call it vanity. It is they who are vain. I succumb in statue. Conceivably she has power over me yet. The goddess has made invisible the solid.

2.

"I who turn to love", she whispers away from your exposed corpse on the soft marble floor or your figure in the doorway, "I who turn to love in endurance of flight and the plunging praise imagine a greater invisible whole." She murmurs in grace of breath as you collapse, cupping blood or tears in an outstretched hand, "As the fulfillment of desire obscures our preordained abandonment, and all other action is false, I have allowed the vibrations of the tenuous apparent world to resound within my hollow chest."

You scream for her to recede from the open window. Perhaps she hears instead your dying cry.

"Yet even that is not enough. My unrealities of exceeding perfection make me less real with each lighter sigh," while she turns to you, "and at present all I see in front of me is the acid-treated cracks in sleeping Cupid's tender hold of the mirror."

Blood seeps from between your foaming lips as you attempt to mutter, "no."

"You are wrong to find consummation in your living creations or impositions; it not a wall or mirror that separates you, but a precipice. Watch me now. Our gaze is unraveling."

Her arms rise and the wind whispers at her cheek. You think maybe a week or a year later that she promises you eternity.

"It has been said that the arrow flying from the bow becomes more than itself once released. Only the oldest master offers the cause."

You couldn't see her fall.

Though at the precise moment she landed in the dumpster, many blithe strangers observed white doves ascend.

No one stopped.
No one noticed a *more intimate flight.*

3.
¿Qué hay detrás del espejo?

Evan Coral
Santa Fe, NM

14

"At Your Service," Sing the Streetlights

"Alright, I have two Big Macs, extra sauce, 40 chicken McNuggets, three large fries, three McChickens, extra mayo, two large cokes, four apple pies, a parfait and a Snickers McFlurry, will that be all for you this evening?"

"Ya, that's it."

"Alright, that'll be $36.50, please pull up to the next window."

"Cool."

Maurice flicked his headset's mouthpiece up to his temple and massaged his eyes slowly with his palms. 4:00 a.m. They always come at 4:00 a.m. They always take ten minutes to order and then the line gets backed up and you're working your ass off, taking orders, going orders, running window to window, trying to be nice, trying to keep the gears churning, the smell of grease and some perverted runner's high keeping you awake while you juggle burgers, cokes, apple pies and courtesies. Saturday night, the great meat-pumping machine at 4:00 a.m. And these guys always keep a monkey wrench handy.

Maurice watched from the drive-through window as the black Mercedes slowed to a stop behind the next car: third in line. Mr. Saturday Night spilled out of the back, driver-side door wearing a salmon button-down tucked into a pair of khakis and a shiny, leather belt. He nearly ripped it all apart some ten feet from the car so he could piss on a tree. The driver watched his boss waddle to the car and crawl in the backseat.

When the car pulled up Maurice talked fast, bracing for impact.

"Alright, I have two Big Macs, extra sauce, 40 chicken McNuggets, three large fries, three McChickens, extra mayo, two large cokes, four apple pies, a parfait and a Snickers McFlurry, is that correct?"

"Whooo, Ronnie, *man,* Ronnie, turn down the music."

The driver smiled and said, "right away, sir," with a thick Jamaican accent. When he smiled, the shine off his teeth could probably be seen from space.

"Whooo, okay. Did you turn it down, Ronnie? Okay, good, okay. Ya, sorry, what was that boss?"

"Is that order correct?"

"You...you got it boss," the man said, suppressing a belch.

"Alright, that'll be $36.50."

"Here Ronnie, give 'em this...they'll love it."

He flicked the credit card at the windshield and began to cackle, falling sideways in the backseat and sprawling.

"Here you go, sir," said Ronnie, handing the card to Maurice, Backseat still cackling. Maurice left the war-zone for the safe glow of the kitchen. He turned to Jorge.

"Hey, you got that big order yet?"

"Almost. Sandra's got the nuggets."

"Right here, Mo."

Sandra handed him a paper bag stuffed with two rectangular packages, hot and pungent and steamy and full of chicken nuggets. A royal parade of identical bags lead into Ronnie's gloved hands, bag after bag after bag of fried and salted American glory. It became a celebration. The drive-through line got longer and longer.

"Thanks, have a good night."

"Thank you, sir," said Ronnie.

"Hey, hold up a second, I got a third Big Mac, there's only two here. Ronnie, didn't I get another Big Mac?"

"I would imagine you did, sir," said Ronnie, smiling in the rearview. He never stopped smiling.

"Ya, can I get another Big Mac?"

"Sorry, I didn't think you ordered one. See, it's not here," and Maurice showed him the receipt.

"Well you took it down wrong, could you get another, boss? Here you go."

Backseat threw his arm out the window, waving a twenty like a young toddler waving a rubber spoon. Maurice took it and looked back at Jorge.

"Jorge, can I get a Big Mac."

"What? You kidding? Same guy wants another Big Mac?"

"*Jorge,* can I get another Big Mac?"

Jorge started another Big Mac.

Backseat talked spiritedly at Ronnie about the girl he went to bed with last weekend, you know, the brunette. Ronnie remembered, "I remember, sir, of course." Sounded like a *night*. Meanwhile, Maurice looked behind the Mercedes at all the cars waiting. Customers drummed their fingers on their steering wheels; the lucky ones could laugh and talk with their friends, but words were few and far between. Some looked like they may have died while waiting for their Big Macs. No one should be here at 4:00 a.m., and yet, with each minute spent on *this* Big Mac, another car got in line.

Maurice brought the boxed and bagged burger to the window, finding Backseat's arms waiting this time. He pulled it into the car and took a quick look in the bag.

"This is wrong! I didn't want cheese...or pickles...no *pickles!* That's what I said...it's not that...hard guys. Ronnie, ask bossman for one a' these without the cheese. Without the cheese!"

"Could we get one without the cheese, sir?" He shrugged at Maurice, still smiling, still gleaming, like a parent talking to the bicycle salesman while their kid tears down the store.

Maurice almost asked him why he would like cheese and pickles on the first two burgers, but not the third. He immediately thought better of it. Maurice did not expect a coherent answer, and either way, he would rather make one burger than three.

"Sir," said Maurice, "maybe I could get you a knife and we could scrape it off? It's going to take us a while to make another one and there's a lot of people behind you."

Backseat stared at Maurice. Ronnie smiled in the rearview, fascinated. After searching the burger box for clues and finding none, Backseat looked up again at Maurice. His eyes carried massive bags, bags that could have carried his drive-through order times twenty. They had trouble focusing. They may have been looking in different directions. Backseat tilted his head a little and opened his mouth like a big cave.

"But...I didn't get it with cheese!"

"Well, it's gonna take a while, are you sure?"

"Well, we got all night, don't we, Ron?"

"Of course, sir."

"Alright, hold on a second--Jorge, I need another Big Mac. No cheese, no pickles."

"What the fuck, man."

An eternity passed again. Customers got out of their cars to walk around. One man--something like a man--single-handedly held up the entire line for a good fifteen minutes. Now, he sang to himself, "one a' these without the cheese, one a' these without the cheese..."

Jorge finished making Big Mac: no cheese, no pickles. Maurice got the burger box and the bag together when he heard a ripping sound like a chainsaw starting up behind him.

"Ooooooh, no no no, man. Don't you do it."

"Fuggi' I'm gon' spit in his shi'." Said Jorge through a tempest of saliva. Some of it even dropped onto his uniform.

"I say let him do it. Fuck this guy, Mo."

"Can you guys keep quiet? Dude, you can't spit in his food, that's crazy."

"We godda teach thi' foo' a lesso', ma'."

"Dude, he can't learn a lesson. He's never gonna learn. He finds that spit in his food, he's not going, 'oh man, I was a dick wasn't I?' Hell no, man, he's comin back an getting us fired, that's what he's doing, and after that who's gonna pay the rent? Sandra, can you back me up here?"

"I don't care as long as he gets out of my sight."

"You can't spit in his food, man. Just let it go."

Jorge looked at the sandwich, defeated, handed it to Maurice, still looking down at the floor. Maurice boxed it, bagged it, smiled it, thanked-for-waiting and handed it to Ronnie, who have it to Backseat. The change for the twenty soon followed.

"Thanks boss, sorry for the...trouble. Hey Ronnie, take me home alright?"

"Right away, sir," smiling.

"Mmmm, say it again."

"Right away, sir."

"Oh, one more."

"Right away, sir."

"For the people in the back!"

"Right away, sir."

"One more fucken time, Ron-nay!"

"Right away, sir."

Backseat hollered like he were watching a rodeo, Ronnie tipped his hat and Maurice watched them drive away.

"Ronnie, are we almost there?"

"We're almost there, sir."

"When, Ronnie? When...will we be there?"

"Right away, sir."

"Alright...one more time...my man."

"Right away, sir."

The car hummed softly over the Tarmac.

"Right away, sir."

"Great...great...great..."

Ronnie looked up at the rearview, smiling.

His boss was asleep, half a chicken McNugget glued to his bottom lip. Ronnie chuckled to himself and turned on the classical

station: Clare de Lune. The black Mercedes
disappeared beneath the shadow of library
tower.

John Rockwell
Los Angeles, CA

Mind You Don't

"Mind you don't trip on Mina," she said but I
would never not see Mina the cat, if she was a cat as
big as me she would hold me on her furry lap and
hug me and I would hug her back not like all those
people I can't touch who won't touch me. Ever
won't touch, or hug. No, I would not mind Mina.
Mina is in my mind whenever I see her or
sometimes just feel her on her way to me, and we
have the same stomach, always wanting more but
our paws swatted down until we try to be in the
mind of those others: please give us more, more,
more. "Now, Lucy, don't get agitated," she will say
or he will say or someone and I wrap my skin up
tight like a bandage around me and my head is big
and round and hot and burns inside like my hand
on the stove. "I told you not! I told you not!"
everyone all my life has been saying: not, not, not.
Not, not, not. Not, not, not, not, not. No. But I love
the work that makes us sit together like stringing
and snapping beans they just keep coming into the
bowl as soon as they leave until they are all gone.
"Don't eat too many of those, Lucy," she says and I
want to tell her that I am not eating them they are
just suddenly in my mouth. But like always my
words won't come out except the first ones that huff

26

with spit all around them: "I . . . I . . . I . . ." is all
even though the others are lined up behind my
mouth pushing and shoving to get to the front to
say what I forgot. Sometimes one perfect one comes
out yesterday or forever ago the zinnias in the
garden so stiff and stemmed like okra hard to cut
but then in the evening in the dark vase like the
picture so happy, so "pretty," I say and "yes they
are" she says but I don't know if she is my mother
or my brother's wife but she smiles and I would hug
but not, not, not, you hug too hard. Now that she is
sick there is always water rushing through my chest
like a spring flood and when I see my brother's face
or hers or my mirror face my head is full of thunder
so much can't they hear? I want to roar at night
tears knife my face I step back inside my body to get
away from my eyes but they won't stop I put the
pillow over my head. Not, not, not, not, not. I try to
help I burn things on the stove and cut my fingers.
"It's all right," she says and her cool hand rises and
falls on the quilt. "Just sit still here with me," she
says, "and everything will be fine. I just need to
rest." Maybe she is my sister, all her words are soft
and she sleeps and I watch and that is what I do
best to watch and make it safe to sleep so there
won't be any more not knowing what to do but I
can't watch all the time. Mina comes with me come

here Mina and we sit on the side porch where shade
is at noon and afternoon and there are old books
there I saw her reading one time what are those she
told me "food for thought" and when I see them I
feel the sharp bellyache of the raw beans that got in
my mouth so I had to eat them but it's worse than
that now there's something like death in those
books I am glad I can't read I don't know what they
might do. Others have died and smelled like lilies or
like ice milk and people bring flowers that already
smell like the dead and close them up forever but
these books smell like ashes. She will not die I will
not let her and not to let her while she sleeps I sit
here penning blue ink in every O in all these books
so the words behind them can't get out and they
will make a fence around us so we stay inside until
we can sit together with big bowls on our laps full of
things to do and listen for him coming back from
the fields or the mill. "Oh, oh, oh," I heard her say
once and bent to see the cutworms in the ear of
corn and it is bad and they are endless but as long
as I am doing death is not happening. As I fill them
in they are black and I am blue and sometimes I
wash up onto the lip of them like hot water in a pan
I carry from the sink to the stove or carried or will
carry the water swinging from one side to the other
it just has to stop. But it is cool now and almost so

dark I cannot see. I can feel Mina's sleep in her head and now it's in mine I can't stop it drifting in from the sick room the fever of sleep she will not I will not let her. And dark washes up to the lip of the world and pours over everything I have done all the mouths I have closed and their ears through which they would suck our breath out if we spoke to them but we won't say anything now we'll just wait and see.

S.C. Bobo
Albany, CA

Wilting

She wakes you (and you catch a glimpse of
the clock—3 am) to smell the wadded sheets
she holds to your face, the sheets she had been
wrapped in where she had fallen asleep on the
floor of the unfinished nursery.

Does this smell like piss? she asks, the
dampness shaky against your cheek.

What? No, honey. You sniff. No, why?
Should it?

All the drive you are silent. And she is silent,
but for her forced exhalations. A nest of tissues
you haphazardly grabbed (when you should
have grabbed a towel) beneath her soaking.

You don't know what to say. You should
have had eight more weeks to think about it, to
prepare. And now something warm and not
unlike fear fills the space inside the car.

The nurses are wheeling her and you follow,
answering questions that you don't quite hear.
The fluorescent hospital lights disorient you;
the chemical sterility about the hallway

31

(stretching, stretching endlessly) spawns a nausea that moves from your gut to your heart, past your throat and into your head.

You sweat, dampness against your chest cold in the chill of the delivery room. An eternity of breathing. You're breathing with her. The chirps and buzzes of machines and numbers on screens scramble your thoughts. She is breathing, you are breathing, and it is loud, getting louder.

Her hand tight clasping yours.

An eternity.

The room suddenly a whitewashed tile vacuum. Silence.

A white-coated doctor holding the grey mass as it darkens purple—bruised by the air. Its mouth stretched open silent screaming, a shrill ring in your ears.

It's handed to her, is in mother's hands and you caress a gentle finger along the soft scalp, your urgency incoherent and white hot through your body as the doctor shoulders in, takes the blue-flesh mass and is gone, the nurse holding you back, telling you sit, it's going to be alright.

And so you sit, waiting, breathing.

An eternity.

You walk her through the hospital's automatic doors and into the sunlight. She limply holds a bouquet of flowers in her hands. There are no more tears—she is empty.

All the drive you are silent. And she is silent, but for her forced inhalations. You try not to blink for the image of the grey mass behind glass and spread tube-fed in its space ship incubator like a specimen prepared for dissection. Something cold and not unlike fear fills the space inside the car.

For days you prepare dinner in silence, set the table for two. The flowers you have arranged in her grandmother's glass vase, and have placed them center table. They are wilting.

Upstairs, you find her asleep, wrapped in wrinkled sheets on the floor of the unfinished nursery. You wake her; lead her downstairs and

into the kitchen, where at the sight of the
flowers her eyes fill to brim without spilling.

   You pull her chair out, and tell her sit, sit,
please, eat.

Heath William
Long Beach, CA

this is how babies die

I woke up this morning before my alarm woke up.

My three cats were asleep beside me. They looked like Orion's Belt but if Orion's Belt were made outta cats.

I liked looking at them, my cats.

I felt like I coulda looked at them forever except I knew I couldn't look at them forever because, if I did, if I did look at them forever, I woulda been really, really late for work.

I rolled outta bed only wearing boxers.

I felt sexy.

I wondered if my asterism cats thought I looked sexy too.

I hope so, I thought to myself. *Guys like "feeling pretty" too.*

After just standing around in my boxers for a little bit, I realized my three cats were all too asleep to give me any potential compliments, so I opened my dresser drawer and took out a new pack of ankle-high, black socks.

Fuck yes! Fuck yes, man! I fuckin' love new socks! I thought to myself.

"Partay on your feet!"

That's what I call wearing new socks because that's what wearing new socks feels like (And fuck you if you don't get at least moderately excited when wearing new socks. We could never be friends if you don't. We're just too different...).

The socks were all connected to this flimsy strip of cardboard packaging. I ripped the socks apart from their cardboard packaging but this small piece of t-shaped plastic got stuck in the toe-region of one of the socks. It was caught/somehow tangled on a thin, singular thread coming undone from the sock and, as much as I tried, I couldn't free the sock from the thread and began getting frustrated in the process of trying to do so.

This is how babies die, I thought to myself.

I began laughing out loud. The thought made absolutely no sense in regards to what I was doing. It was like a thought I was supposed to have about something else a long time ago but, instead, the thought arrived to my brain really, really, really late and when I was getting ready for work on the day of June 17th, 2014 and when I couldn't get a small t-shaped piece of plastic unstuck from one of my new black socks that I was totally bonered up to wear to work and when I wasn't doing/seeing something that was even remotely threatening towards the life of an infant.

This is how babies die, I repeated over and over inside my head. The thought was like some bizarre, internally-spoken lullaby that was keeping me awake in this elevated state of consciousness where everything was okay and nothing hurt because there was nothing to be hurt over, rather than letting me fall asleep and, therefore, sink back into my usual frame of mind where everything was bad and where everything was painful and where I always found ways, no matter how good things actually were, to create some kinda suffering for myself.

This is how babies die...

I was still laughing as I finally freed the piece of plastic from my sock.

I got dressed.

I smelled pancakes with syrup even though I knew I was the only one awake and, therefore, no one was cooking them. I went to the kitchen just to make sure.

No pancakes, though.

No fuckin' pancakes...

Typical...

Whatever.

This is how babies die...

When I was in the kitchen, I looked through the window and saw two empty crock-pots on a table on our deck. They had been left out over night without their lids on after having been used at a family party the day before and they had both been rained on and were filled to their brims with water.

This is how babies die, I said to myself, shaking my head while looking at the crock-pots left out overnight. Then I laughed and grabbed a Peach Diet Snapple and left.

On my way to work, I listened to a Motion City Soundtrack playlist. There were so many dead deer in the road/on the side of the road that morning I began counting them on my forty-five minute drive. Whenever I sped through a yellow light that was on the verge of turning red, I thought, *This is how babies die...*

to myself and then I always smiled. It made my speeding through yellow lights even more enjoyable than usual.

And four.

Four was the total amount of dead deer I spotted on my way to work.

It was me, an ex-Marine, a twenty-two year old ginger with thick-rimmed, black glasses and a cute but married technician at work that day. It was a Sunday, and the hospital was closed on Sundays, and so only a few of us were needed to take care of the animals we had in the hospital.

The cute but married technician took care of the cats in the cat room (which I didn't like because I liked taking care of the cats in the cat room) and myself and the other two kennel workers took care of all the dogs in the kennel.

There were about twelve dogs or so. First we walked them all. Then the ginger fed them as the ex-Marine cleaned bowls and racks and as I cleaned cages.

"I bet I'm wearing the newest socks outta everyone here today," I said while removing piss soaked newspaper from one of the small, top cages like some kinda weird vacuum with hands.

"Haha, what?" asked the ex-Marine, lining up all of the bowls he had cleaned to dry.

"How new are you socks?" I asked him.

"Haha, I dunno, man. Not very new. I mean, they don't have holes or anything in them but, ya know..."

"I knew it! I knew I had the newest socks here! I put these mother fuckers on this morning. They feel great. Fuckin' partay on my feet!"

The ex-Marine laughed. The ginger with thick-rimmed, black glasses was too busy/focused feeding the dogs to pay attention to me.

I didn't care.

I knew I had her beat.

I knew my socks were newer than hers.

"Hey, Meg."

"What?" the ginger with thick-rimmed, black glasses replied.

"Did you walk Crumb?"

"Yeah, why?"

"You forgot to give him water."

"Haha, oops..."

I sighed overdramatically. "This is how babies die, you guys..." I said, shaking my head. "This is how fuckin' babies die..."

The two of them laughed.

I laughed.

The truth is funny.

Truth in comedy.

After cleaning up lots more shit and piss, we all finished up and went home. I thought about marshmallows on my drive back and pondered the simple yet authentic happiness they brings into people's lives. I also recounted all of the dead deer I saw in the road/on the side of the road.

Four.

Still four dead deer.

No more casualties.

Some things never change.

When I walked into my bedroom, my cats didn't look like Orion's Belt anymore. One was lying on the bed, another on the floor, and the other off somewhere I couldn't see.

This kinda scattered belt would never hold Orion's belt up... Scattered belts are how babies die.

I lied down in bed with my clothes on.

I felt sexy even though I wasn't only in my boxers.

I felt calm and peaceful.

I felt myself in this rare state of heightened awareness where I was physically able to see the emptiness we all shared and lived in together, and how simple life was when you were able to look at this emptiness and have it look at you in return.

One of my cats began purring. I listened to him purr and began thinking, *This is how babies die...* over and over to myself until I fell asleep.

I dreamed a series of dreams, a TV mini-series of dreams, but I don't remember what they were about.

If my dreams were turned into a TV mini-series, I wonder if people woulda watched them.

Tom Hanks.

People would totally woulda watched them if we got Tom Hanks to star in them.

People will watch Tom Hanks in anything. He's captivating.

Calvero
Trumbull, CT

In the Shade

Hot dogs sizzle on the grill. The picnic table is littered with paper plates, plastic cups and a carton of orange juice. A toy horse stands next to the bottle of Vodka on the table. I pretend the horse has galloped up to a crystal castle. My dad says the horse is for me, but it has to stay here when I go home. I don't want to play with the horse if it isn't mine, but there is nothing to do when I'm at my dad's house. The day is heating up.

I am in the shade of the stucco house watching my dad and his girlfriend play badminton on the back lawn. Kelley wears shorts and a macramé bikini top, her hair streaked sunlight blonde.

My mom has been teaching me how to macramé. We are making things like plant hangers and trivets. If I asked to make a macramé bikini top, she would say no because they are not modest.   Kelley is not modest.

Kelley smiles a lot and begins every exclamation with "Christ!" She doesn't go to

46

church. I know this because I asked her what church she goes to.

"Oh Christ," she exclaims, smiling so big that she shows her gums, "Not everybody goes to church. I don't buy into organized religion, you know?"

I nod, uncomfortable, not sure what she means. I keep quiet hoping she'll explain, but she doesn't. I am pretty sure she doesn't like me, but I don't know why.

"Go on and play with Kelley," my dad says, handing me his racquet as he goes to the grill. He is turning the hot dogs and taking long drinks out of a plastic cup. Kelley is waiting by the net, jiggling the birdie in her palm and bouncing on the balls of her bare feet.

I don't want to play because it's Sunday and I am supposed to Keep The Sabbath Day Holy. I miss being at church with my friends. I shake my head no and stay on the patio.

My dad shrugs. "Suit yourself, kid," he says as he finishes his drink and strolls over to Kelley. She has taken off her macramé bikini top and he is kissing her in the sunshine. They call it Frenching, and they pass a sweet smelling cigarette back and forth, holding their breath, then smiling and smiling.

Kelley laughs, swatting his bottom with her racquet. I hate it when they take off their clothes. My dad laughs at me and says I am uptight, just like my mom. For a minute I think he is going to get mad, but he doesn't. He just stares at me and explains that it's good to be natural, that there is nothing to be ashamed of. I watch them, naked and grinning, laughing at me. I don't know why being like my mom is considered a bad thing, but I know I feel embarrassed by them.

"Christ, she keeps staring at me," Kelley says to my dad in a low voice, glancing at me. Turning away.

I twirl the racquet like a baton, acting like I don't hear her. I am humming hymns under my breath. I am staying in the shade.

Erin Parker
Long Beach, CA

49

Not Named

In this small bathroom the walls are a grid of cloudy gray squares. The walls crowd against this porcelain white tub, and the clear silver water rises, rises. Her body is here. The slender back rests along the curve of the tub and the elbows slouch mid thigh and the arms are like two L's— I trace the outline, and wonder about this face hidden behind a book. I am hesitant and eager to tell her something as I sit on the edge of the bathtub watching her read.

But it is so hard to describe a place you're not actually at. You're being there is like squinting into the sun, like peering into a fog so bright with sun you could be anywhere at all. So you tell yourself a story, you locate the body like a finger on a map, but you're map is like a dream, it collects the dust and water around you, shaping the mold this way and that way. You're being there, which is to say here, in this bathroom, is like remembering being here, only you're forgetful and distracted.

Look, she says, your hairs are dripping;
there are strings of water falling from the tip of
your penis. I can see underneath, your
wrinkles, your flesh, and the tuffs of curled
hairs. I smile at her, thinking on the edge of
this tub, or this cliff edge. I contemplate her
paired eyes—two brown moons that peer
through a telescope an island away. I am
watched, my sex is hers, she scrutinizes my
scrotum, and I am on the other side of a vast
space of air.

Where am I? Where were we? My mouth
tastes salty and dry as I breathe. Salty because I
am here and there, remembering, reaching out
to this one with a single hand, the one who
amuses herself by my sudden hardening— a
crane lifting, a wave breaking, the Eiffel tower,
a massive index finger— reaching out much
farther with another hand, tense and calm as a
knife on a neck.

This hand is connected to that other side of a
vast space of air. This air is salty, not of the
bathroom. Somewhere, miles away, there's a

sky heavy on the shoulders of a girl. I can feel my stomach rumbling for her now. She is a conversation waiting to speak out against my betrayal, and I am hungry for her words. I feel immense responsibility; I could take care of her with my listening because her voice is not her body, though the body churns the voice. And somewhere, miles away, a coastline hisses and purrs like a bored cat, like a band of sick cats lounging on grand pianos, and their noises are the waves breaking on the sand.

I have nothing to say, to either worlds. I the slightest movement of two worlds. I am the remembering and recalling of her (the other), my movements are her brisk and helpless stumbles, and I am also her bathtub sea horizon, this one, the one here, fogged over; I am a field of circular ripples, the rolling from her skin toward the white edges of this circular tub-seashore. I am these rings upon rings, held and holding, as I sit on the edge of this ivory white tub.

Look me in the eyes, hear this, she says:
Doubt thou the stars are fire; Doubt that the
sun doth move; Doubt truth to be a liar; But
never doubt I love. I think about my penis,
about books and movies, and a man who once
wrote about looking down at his own penis,
and how beautiful he felt for being inside his
someone twice that day.

I repeat and recall the images of the
bathroom as if to center myself into quiet
speaking— a box of Marlboros, cloudy bushes
of smoke, tiny cylinders of ash, her
picturesque, cyclical breathing. I am hard. I am
pulled out from her ankles or thighs as if some
great, invisible spirit, a puppeteer of air, were
pulling each of my selves from her skin with
magical strings. Why am I thinking, and not
speaking? Why am I a ripple and a speculation?
Oh, that damned phrase, the only real thought:
Es konnte auch anders sein— don't tempt me, I
am about to speak to you, the one here, the one
scrutinizing:

The moon is the most alive thing on this earth.

What do you mean by alive?

I don't know.

How big is the core of the earth?

Why do you ask?

I don't know.

How did the ancients explain the waves?

I don't know.

Does the moon move the waves? Do the waves move the moon? Is the core of the earth hot as the sun? Is the full moon only a misnomer since the fullness is only half the moon, since the half-fullness is only at the surface?

They believed in eye diseases too.

Who?

The ancients.

Receding tides like slick, reptilian skin, skin pulled and braided into rope. Her big toe lifts, turns off the facet. The column of water ceases, and the tub grows nearly flat. The shower current is hanging from metal loops scrunched into eggshell colored folds. The walls' tiles are little cloudy gray squares. I am pale allover, and my head is resting against my left knee. I have skin that might be softer if I was like her.

In the bathroom, I thought about having sex together. I thought maybe we would both feel a sudden urge, and do it right there on the cold, gray floor. She would be wet with bathwater, and I would slip against her body before her skin turned dry and stuck to mine. We, of course, wouldn't finish. Instead, side-by-side, on our backs, our eyelids pressed tight together, we would finish ourselves, collect our things, and then walk up the stairs to bed, to warm sleep that doesn't remember or forget,

that doesn't remember or forget to be alone or
not.

Jamison Gilmour
Culver City, CA

57

Bask

"Turn and look at me". He says this with desperation. I cannot meet his gaze. It is burning a hole into the side of my face. His constant question, "What is wrong?" I don't know how to answer anymore. It used to be so easy to make up some bullshit lie like having watched a commercial about starving children in Africa or Brooklyn - I switch between the two - or a distant memory from my lonesome childhood triggered by our box of cereal. Nowadays I do not have the energy to create. The reality has set in. There is no reason for my constant daydreaming or never having a worthwhile word to say at dinner. My body has taken to automatically reverting to autopilot. Floating around I look down and am reminded my legs still work.

   I sigh in relief; he has retreated in frustration to our bedroom. The slam of the door makes me jump. I know I should follow but I have been sitting on the couch for hours and have made too much of a comfortable dent to leave.

I have come to accept a certain ritual. Upon waking I sit and look out my favorite window. It is curtained with a sheer crushed material. I can see the world but the world is unaffected by my despondent stare. I feel safe in this sort of hiding, yet terrified in my time sitting with my self. The world, or at least the street I watch, is constant, dreary, and dead or alive. Panes of glass break up the window. A scene neatly chopped up, the way entomologists tell us flies see the world. Allowing the brain to do what it does best, make a whole from parts. I read that people affected by autism notice specifics before they see a whole. That is the way I look through my window, slowing moving my gaze from one pane to the next. Sometimes seeing the whole is overwhelming but I am king at avoidance.

I can hear the TV in the bedroom. He will soon fall asleep, always easy for him to escape into his dreams. I should not hold that against him but somehow I find myself guilty of envy, one of five deadly sins.

I am young, he many years older. Yet it is I who announced that I was committed for life. I was set; I wanted to look nowhere else for love. A conclusion more appropriate out of his wise and lived mouth. I did not have the energy for heartbreak. Now it seems that I am the one closer to the finish line.

This ritual is my blanket. I know what I am doing when I don't talk or move. The observant, that I am. His frustration is a lullaby. The repetitive sound of his shaky words bound for my heart, or whatever is in there. They say I bask in my own shit. I mutter a no, my shit is what I know and there lives the fear of ever leaving. I sit at my desk waiting for the continuation of my lullaby. He walks in from work. At first it is polite concern, then with haste his words of resentment make my eyelids heavy, heavy with guilt. I gather the throw next to me as safety. A door slams shut. The obvious repetition of a life wasted makes for a good nap. Nothing like 'Itsy Bitsy Spider', this feeble try is for adults.

Michael Johnson
Arcadia, CA

The Space on the Top of My Shoulder

He sits listening for his name among the other applicants. The chair is a dark grey, ultra-modern low back species that is shockingly comfortable. It's of the cheaper sort, not leather, but a rough material made for the expectation of heavy use in the sterile and inhospitable waiting rooms of modern office buildings having the texture that can best be described as 'cat's tongue.' It's also the kind where the rubber supports stretch as you sit. The longer you're there the more it goes so that with any repositioning of weight, the chair lets out a strangely accurate fart sound throughout the open area, echoing off the acoustically ideal heavy glass and gleaming hard tiled floors. This leaves him to look around trying to avoid embarrassment by taking a sudden rational view of things as if he were trying to diagram the various areas of physics and auditory ricochets needed to produce such a sound in such a space at such a volume while others are left to look at him, though knowing, because they are in the same faux-designer chairs, that it was not what it sounded like but still wondering if it wasn't the exception and monitoring the slowly circulating air for any subtle hints of methane with the assumed precision of sommeliers after the master exam while still looking at him like he was some hack flatulist who couldn't make it in the cut-throat world of fart comedy. It reminds him of college when it would be late and he would hear the sound of compressing bed springs in broken, start-stop rhythm and couldn't be sure if it was what he thought it was, but he had already started thinking of it and knew that he wouldn't be able to keep eye contact with his neighbor the next morning. As in that case and this one, he kept his head down and avoided all eye contact and while waiting to be called engrossed himself in some series of papers that have nothing relevant to add to his interview. It is to look aggressive without having anything to be aggressive with. In the wild it's called puffery, not to be confused with fluffing which is another thing all together and characteristic of those creatures indigenous to the San Fernando Valley. He looks up quickly and sees the tactic working as they stop caring if he was the carpet bomber, which he wasn't and they know it, and go back, considering the economy they are living through, being pitted against each other, willing to Game of Throne each other, to the serious shit of interviewing for this job.

A woman walks out of the opaque doors and approaches the reception desk across from the waiting area, gets her parking validated and leaves with no visible expression, giving nothing those who still await. After a ninety-two second break, he is called and passes through the frosted glass doors where only light escapes leaving him a vague shadow, a figure of a man, walking beyond and out of sight of those left behind.

He takes a seat on the same side of the small conference table in a high back leather chair, identical to the dozen others around the room, with a smooth action in both recline and rotation and begins his interview. For fifteen minutes the boiler plate questions are volleyed with perfunctory answers returned and are not worth retelling but telling nevertheless. He notices that the interviewer had stopped writing and is keeping the pen stationary on the paper. He cannot be sure if the interviewer had written anything.

"Tell me about a difficult problem you faced and how you dealt with it?"

He couldn't think of anything and started talking. "I was almost eighteen, in love, holding five hundred dollars and her name was – is – Isabel." He rose out of the chair, removed his jacket, and rolled up his sleeve. "See, it takes up the space below my elbow, here on the inside of the forearm and was impossible to cover up...We were together for two years," he took his seat, turned toward the interview, rested his left arm on the desk, and leaned forward, "in high school. I got it before we graduated and before summer's end she was gone and we were broken up. She went to Vassar, I knew she was, but I thought it wouldn't matter. I understand – now- why she did so in a letter – not that it was ok– and that she must've felt good being on the other side of the country. But there I was, a tattooed moron. I should've known not to get it when the artist refused to do it – at first. He asked me who Isabel was and I lied. I told him it was my mother and she was sick and roses were her favorite flower. I went on about how I wanted her to see it as soon as possible. I don't think he believed it. I know he believed that I would take the five hundred dollars to another shop. He told me to sit. Gave me a book of tattoos. Turned to the section with flowers. Asked which one I liked. Drew the sketch. Fired up the gun and charged me five hundred dollars.

"The first year at UCLA was tough but a breakthrough came in my second year. It was early in the fall quarter, a good amount of student loan money, and a better amount of Jack and Coke from playing the Wiki drinking game.

"The what?"

"It's simple. You say something that you don't think is in Wikipedia, and if it's not there everyone else drinks, if wrong, you drink. You'd be surprised what people put on Wikipedia...But the breakthrough came when I went looking for the janitor's closet for an electric sander to scrap it off. I didn't find the closet or anything suitable and eventually fell out in the showers on the fifth floor of Hendrick Hall – top of the hill as it's called. It was also the night I learned the irrefutable truth that you never know how drunk you are until you stand up.

"The next day at lunch, I met a friend who said I should go the other way with it. He suggested that I get the whole arm with every girl I've known that way it would blend together and one wouldn't matter more than the rest. I didn't take the advice as such. Instead, on the space below Isabel – see – is Alicia. She was my first girlfriend. I like how the ribbon comes across the lower part and how the script came out clean. The vine that winds around my forearm connecting them, along with the leaves and shading I did later. But it could not have been done without healthy contributions from FAFSA. It was an education expense on the Socratic, paideia-esque level. That's not discounting the subsequent Hep-C scare and skin infection.

"It was almost a full year after that I met Alison. You're going to have to take my word for it. I can't roll the sleeve up any farther. I was living in Santa Monica and she was majoring in art history and finance. Before the spring quarter was over we got a one bedroom apartment on 11th Street, south of Wilshire, near the Tommy's Burger on Lincoln. She asked about it on the first date and I told her the story. It always comes up early in conversation. She seemed indifferent to the whole thing but never told me to not get another. She had to know that I would get another with her name on it and never said anything to stop it. It takes most of the front and outside of my bicep. It's the Maid of Orleans, the national flower of the Philippines. I might not have done it if she said anything. I realized that was the point. Do you see? I had never asked any of them whether I should or if they wanted me to. It was something I was doing for myself as much as them. It was a – it is a – living concatenated display of those women I've loved – love. It wasn't something to regret. The initial feeling I had when I was eighteen was gone. I have been lucky that the ones I've loved have not done anything terrible to make it painful after it was over. But had they, I've thought about this a lot, if one of them had hurt me badly, it wouldn't take away from what made me get it. In that case, the bad would be something if not worth remembering, would be necessary to remember and I would not want to forget that it happened - the good or the bad.

"I saw Alison a year ago when she came to visit from Seattle. We met at Versailles. She loves Cuban food...or more accurately, she loves fried plantains. But who doesn't love fried plantains? We talked about what had happened since college and about how we would drive from the apartment twice a week to this place learning the side streets to avoid traffic on Venice and Washington only to stay past rush hour drinking mojitos at the and being seriously drunk by the time we ate.

""Let me see it," she said."

""Just look under the table.""

"She called me immature and I rolled the short sleeve up to my shoulder. She said when she first saw it that she was half sorry and half something she couldn't define. We had a year together after I got it and I remember it has sweet and easy with only thinking about classes and getting the rent and being with each other. I know it wasn't all that way, but I don't remember it as any other way. Now she said she was glad it existed. 'Existed' was her word. Not glad I got it, but that it existed. She said it was a love letter that she did have but knew where it was. I thought that was the best description of it.

"She saw that there was another above hers. She asked who it was and I told her it had been five years since we broke up and had met someone else. She looked at me in the way she did when equally annoyed and amused and then looked away for as long as it took for me to apologize. Then she said, 'What if we get back together and get married? What happens then?' She said it just to mess with me. Then she asked again. 'Who is Carmen?'

"I didn't tell her much. I only told her that Carmen was beautiful. I didn't feel like telling her anything personal. It could've only soured the time we were having. She asked how we met and I told her that she – Carmen – was in

70

the same grad school program I was in. She asked how serious Carmen and I were. I told her that it was very serious and she let it go after that. I couldn't tell her that I loved Carmen more or that she didn't like the other names and would black them out with a sharpie and in the morning there would be black smudges on the underside of my pillow. But Carmen loved hers and would trace her finger around the edges of it whenever she could. She didn't care that they were my past. If I had told her that they love letters, she would've said that some people burn love letters. I never thought that she would, but I knew she was capable. It also didn't help that she 'accidentally' broke my original pressing of My Aim is True. Although, in her defense, I shouldn't have played it so often...But honestly, there were times when I thought about laser removal...I feel worse about Carmen than the others. It was terrible at the end and it was my fault. A beautiful woman of my own age, caring and beneficent, who loved me more than she should have. That is who Carmen was.

"I suppose all this can be expected from the cause. There were, however, some interesting side effects. The first, which shocked me, was that it made me instantly more interesting to women. Not all, but more than before. It has also started a subtle competition and a desire to get me to tattoo their names atop of the others. I think they like the idea it, of a permanent mark that they don't have to worry or feel guilty over if they decide they don't really like me. It's funny when they think a week is enough – or a night. Like it's an ice breaker where I go out, have some drinks, meet a woman, find a shop, say goodbye and be on to the next one. This appeal has also proved useful in the ending of relationships. After a certain amount of time I know whether I'll get another and if not it's clear that the thing is over. Some of them ask, 'Are you going to put mine there?' as they touch the space on the top of my shoulder. If you have to ask then I'm probably not. Don't be confused, it doesn't make the conversation any easier or them less pissed, but it forces the question where in other relationships they – I mean we – would go along for years because it's the thing to do. It's what people expected and we would like each other enough and have nothing to force us to think otherwise. We'd get married, have kids, and all the rest, because it was too comfortable to leave. Any idea of passion, love, or a little hate would not exist but it's nice to not have to worry about who you will go to a wedding with or take home for Christmas – which based on my observations is the basis of too many relationships. That first tattoo – that first stupid move – has kept me from ever falling into that kind of trouble. Too much gets built around complacency. Not for me. This thing turned out to have been the damned smartest thing I've ever done.

"How long ago was Carmen?" asked the interviewer.

"Two years ago. She was the last one. It fits most of the top of my arm, wrapping around the side and back of the tricep. Now there is a nice place, the space on the top of my shoulder. The next one goes there. "

"Is there anyone?"

"No. Not right now."

"So that's a problem you found yourself in and solved?"

"Yes. Is there anything else?"

"I don't think so. We've been talking in here a bit longer than ideal."

"I look forward to hearing from you."

"Thank you for coming in but...I don't think we'll be calling you back...I don't think you'd fit in with the team mentality we're trying to cultivate."

He goes back to the reception desk, on the other side of the opaque doors, sees the people in the waiting area glancing, taking as much as they can without staring. He takes his ticket and hates himself quietly for having said, "I look forward to hearing from you." He felt like the guy who calls a girl who hasn't called him back and leaves a message asking if this is her correct number. He gets in his car and drives to his apartment in Echo Park.

Chris Camargo
Long Beach, CA